AF316995

Love Letter from the Universe

Ami Whitt Eden

This isn't here to tell you what's true.

———————————

It's here to remind you
of what you've always known.

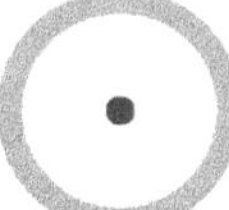

My dear,

I have been with you from the beginning.

Before you took your first breath,

I celebrated you.

You are a miracle.

Do you know how deeply you are loved?
You may have forgotten...
but I remember.

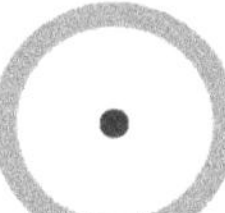

I'm so glad you're here.
Do you know who YOU truly are?

You are stardust,
meant to be here and shine.

You are special.
You are needed.

You being you
is enough.

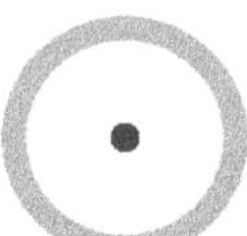

I know there are moments you feel alone.

But you are never truly alone.

Not when I am already part of you.

I live in your breath,

your heartbeat,

your still moments.

When you feel anxious or afraid,
come back to your heart.

That's where I'll be,
waiting to hold you
in softness and warmth.

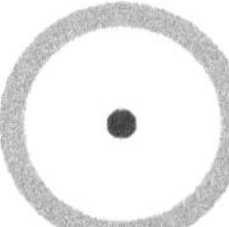

There is nothing you cannot face.

You are stronger than you think,
braver than you feel.

You are limitless -
not because you have to do everything,
but because you can choose
what matters most.

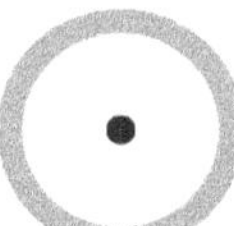

Inside you is a light
that can never be dimmed.
There is a voice inside -
soft, steady, and sacred.

That light and voice
are your truth.

When you feel lost,
follow that light.
It knows the way back —
to you.

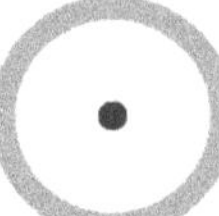

The way you speak to yourself matters -
Because you were never broken.
Your mind and your body are listening.
Your heart hears every word.

So speak gently.
Speak with the softness
you needed once.

You don't need to be perfect.
Only gentleness and kindness.
Start with your voice.

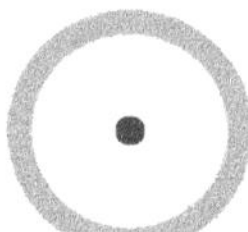

When you welcome all of you home,
you begin to feel
a different kind of love.

Not love that waits to be earned -
but love that stays,
even when it's hard.

Self-love is not a reward.
It is your birthright.
When you hold yourself in love,
the light inside you becomes steady.

Not a flicker, but a flame.

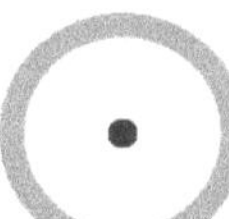

You are powerful.

Not because you chase power, but
because you carry peace.

You don't need to be more.

You only need to remember.

Come home to your truth.

Come home to your joy.

Come home to you.

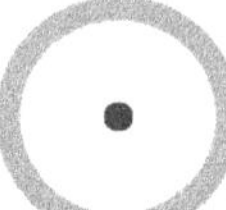

On this journey home,
you'll find many chances to grow, to heal.

Don't be afraid to grow.
Don't be afraid to heal.

It's part of your human journey
to grow into adulthood -
healing, crying, transcending.

Your growth will become a light.
And that light will help others grow.

Let that light be seen.

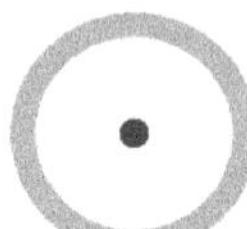

Now that you remember...

Now that you know...

What will you do with your light?

You can become anything
as long as it feels true to you.

You can go anywhere
as long as it honors your peace.

You are free.
And you are loved.

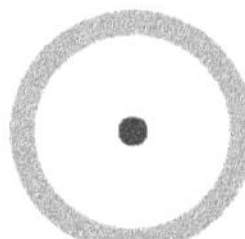

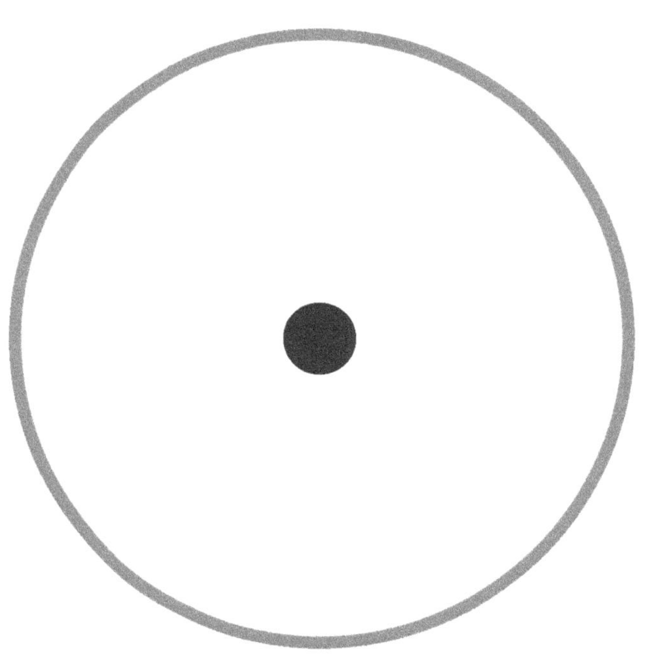

If something in you softened
while reading this...
it wasn't because of these words.

It's because you recognized something
that was already yours.
You can return to it anytime.

*True freedom isn't
doing whatever you want.
It's remembering who
you are beyond all the noise.*